SOJOURNER TRUTH

ABOLITIONIST AND ACTIVIST

"Children, who made your skin white?
Was it not God?
Who made mine Black?
Was it not the same God?
Am I to blame, therefore,
because my skin is Black?"
— Sojourner Truth —

BY LAURA SPINALE

Published by The Child's World®
1980 Lookout Drive • Mankato, MN 56003-1705
800-599-READ • www.childsworld.com

CONTENT CONSULTANT

Mary Butler, former director of the Research Center,
Sojourner Truth Institute

PHOTOS

Cover and page 4: National Portrait Gallery, Smithsonian Institution
Interior: CHINE NOUVELLE/SIPA/Newscom: 27; Collection of the Smithsonian
National Museum of African American History and Culture, Gift from the Liljenquist
Family Collection: 15; Everett Collection/Newscom: 6; Everett Collection/Shutterstock.
com: 22; Glasshouse Images/Newscom: 21, 31; National Portrait Gallery, Smithsonian
Institution: 13, 24, 29; North Wind Picture Archives: 9, 11, 12, 14, 16, 20, 23, 28; Osborn
& Durbec/Library of Congress, Prints and Photographs Division: 8; Roberto Lusso/
Shutterstock.com: 26; Schomburg Center for Research in Black Culture, Jean
Blackwell Hutson Research and Reference Division, The New York Public Library: 5;
Schomburg Center for Research in Black Culture, Manuscripts, Archives, and Rare
Books Division, The New York Public Library: 10; Schomburg Center for Research
in Black Culture, Photographs and Prints Division, The New York Public Library:
7, 19, 25; The Metropolitan Museum of Art, Gift of Mrs. Russell Sage, 1908: 18

LIBRARY OF CONGRESS CATALOGING-IN-PUBLICATION DATA

ISBN 9781503854499 (Reinforced Library Binding)
ISBN 9781503854932 (Portable Document Format)
ISBN 9781503855311 (Online Multi-user eBook)
LCCN: 2021930429

Printed in the United States of America

Cover and page 4 caption:
Sojourner Truth in 1870

CONTENTS

4

Chapter One

EQUAL RIGHTS

Sojourner Truth was an outspoken **abolitionist**. For many years she traveled the country speaking to audiences about the need for slavery to end. In May of 1851, Truth attended the Women's Rights Convention in Akron, Ohio. She was there to support women's equality and the right to vote. Throughout her life, Truth spoke out for equality for women and Blacks.

Sojourner Truth was a good speaker. Her voice was strong and her words were powerful. Audiences remembered what she said to them. At the convention, Truth got up to speak to the supporters of women's rights. Some women had not wanted her to speak. They feared that Truth's antislavery message might confuse the audience. Truth was allowed to speak, however. By the end of her speech, the audience was cheering loudly.

Sojourner Truth
around 1860

The *New York Tribune* first printed the words of Truth's speech. It is quite different from how Gage remembered it. The newspaper's account did not use Black dialect like Gage's did. However, Gage's account is the one most often remembered and quoted in literature.

Years later, women's rights activist Frances Gage recorded Truth's words. The 1851 speech is the one for which Truth is most widely remembered:

That man over there says that women need to be helped into carriages, and lifted over ditches, and to have the best place everywhere. Nobody helps me any best place. And ain't I a woman? Look at me! Look at my arm. I have plowed, I have planted and I have gathered into barns. And no man could head me. And ain't I a woman?

Sojourner Truth, formerly named Isabella, spread the messages of social reform and equality for most of her adult life. Born enslaved, she dedicated her life as a free woman to supporting the rights of all people, especially Blacks and women. She became a well-respected speaker throughout the country. Her words were memorable, and her legacy lives on.

Members of a Black women's organization are pictured in 1900. Many people were inspired by Sojourner Truth and continued her life's work by fighting for social reform and equality.

Chapter Two

A LIFE IN CAPTIVITY

Slavery in the United States began with the first colonies in the 1600s. Enslaved people were forced to work for wealthier people and were often treated cruelly. Their enslavers often beat them. Enslaved people worked many hours and received no pay in return. Their lives were extremely difficult.

Isabella was born into slavery in New York around 1797. She never knew the exact year of her birth. Most enslavers did not keep records of the births or deaths of their workers. Isabella's parents, James and Betsey, were both enslaved. The Hardenbergh family held them in slavery.

A 1784 ad announcing the sale of Black people to be sold into slavery.

Slavery existed in the South on **plantations**. It existed in the North as well. At one time, states such as New York, New Jersey, and Pennsylvania permitted slavery.

Johannis Hardenbergh was said to have treated his workers fairly well. Still, Isabella and her family did not have an easy life. They lived in a small, underground cellar with only one tiny window. Even during the day, the room was almost completely dark. The family slept on wooden boards placed on the cold, damp floor. Water dripped through cracks in the walls when it rained. Sometimes, the ground turned into a big pool of mud.

Isabella was never really sure how many brothers and sisters she had. She never knew most of them. Hardenbergh sold most of her brothers and sisters to other families before Isabella was born. Isabella only knew her younger brother, Peter.

Enslaved people in South Carolina outside of their cabins in 1860.

An enslaved mother and daughter hug as they are sold on an auction block.

Betsey, Isabella's mother, was a **Christian**. She taught Isabella and Peter to pray. Betsey believed that only God could help her family survive. Praying comforted Isabella. It made her feel as though someone was watching over her. Betsey also told Isabella how important it was to obey her enslavers. She promised Isabella that if she was very good, she would be rewarded someday.

Unfortunately, Isabella was soon separated from her family. When she was about 9 years old, Hardenbergh died. His family sold his belongings, including his workers. James and Betsey were too old to sell. The Hardenbergh family decided to set them free. They let them stay in the cold, dark, cellar room. However, Isabella was sold to the Neely family for $100.

Enslaved people were considered their enslavers' property. They were bought and sold at auctions similar to how paintings and other items are bought and sold at auctions today.

Up to this point, Isabella only spoke the Dutch language. (The Hardenberghs were Dutch.) Isabella had never heard English until she was sold to the Neely family. She could not speak a word of English when she first arrived. When the Neelys asked her to do something, she could not understand them. Isabella's new enslavers were cruel to her. They believed she was disobedient or stupid because she could not understand them. John Neely often beat her.

This 1852 illustration shows a male enslaver beating his enslaved worker.

When Isabella learned that her mother had died, she asked for permission to visit her father, James. During this visit, James learned that Neely beat Isabella. James knew that something should be done. He asked a fisherman named Martinus Schryver to buy Isabella. Schryver was a kinder enslaver than Neely.

After about one year, Schryver sold Isabella to the Dumont family. Isabella had a difficult time with her new enslavers. John Dumont occasionally beat her, although not as harshly as Neely had. Dumont's wife did not like Isabella and made her life very difficult. Mrs. Dumont often blamed Isabella for mistakes that other workers had made.

However, Dumont recognized that Isabella was an excellent worker. She could work long and hard. In the mornings, she worked in the fields. At night, she cleaned and did laundry. Dumont said Isabella could do as much farm work as his best male workers.

While working for Dumont, Isabella met a young enslaved man named Robert. He lived on a nearby farm. Robert came to visit Isabella whenever he could. The two made secret plans to marry. When Robert's enslaver found out, he became angry. He told Robert to stop seeing Isabella. The enslaver wanted Robert to marry one of his workers. But Robert and Isabella continued to meet in secret.

An enslaved woman on a sugar plantation in Louisiana

Robert's enslaver soon found out. The next time Robert went to visit Isabella, his enslaver followed him and brutally beat him. Robert finally agreed to marry one of the enslaver's workers. Isabella never saw him again.

Isabella was forced to marry one of Dumont's workers named Thomas. She did not love him, but Isabella had to obey her enslaver. Isabella's first child was born in 1815. She and Thomas had several more children together. Isabella taught all of them to be obedient and honest, just as her mother had taught her. For many years, Isabella continued to work hard for the Dumont family.

An enslaved family doing laundry outside their cabin.

Chapter Three

FREEDOM FOUND

In 1817, New York passed a law that freed enslaved people in the state who were born before 1799. These enslaved people would be freed on July 4, 1827. Since Isabella was born before 1799, she would be freed. However, Dumont and Isabella came to an agreement that he would free her early because of her hard work.

Isabella tried to do everything the Dumont family asked of her. She worked as hard as she could so she could be freed earlier. In 1825, she cut her hand as she worked in the fields. It was a serious injury. For many months, she could not work as hard as she had before.

Sojourner Truth
around 1864

The Van Wagenen family gave Isabella a room in which to sleep. It was the first time she ever slept in a bed.

In 1826, Isabella asked Dumont to set her free as he said he would. He refused. Dumont said that Isabella owed him another year because she had not worked very hard while her hand was injured. Isabella disagreed with Dumont. She believed her hard work throughout all her years with Dumont was enough to keep her end of the agreement. She decided to leave. One morning in late 1826, Isabella woke before dawn and walked away from the Dumonts' property. She carried her youngest daughter, Sophia, with her.

Isabella was now a **fugitive**. She had no money or food. Sophia was still a baby and needed care. Isabella first stopped at the house of Levi Rowe, who was an old friend. He could not help her because he was very sick, but he directed her to the house of the Van Wagenen family. Isabella had known them for some time. They and the Dumonts were members of the same church. Unlike the Dumonts, however, the Van Wagenens were against slavery. The Van Wagenens were kind to Isabella. She was not used to this. All her life, Isabella had been told that Black people were **inferior** to whites. Sometimes, she even believed it. Isabella was shocked that she was finally being treated as an equal.

A fugitive man being captured

Soon, Dumont learned where Isabella was. He tried to force Isabella to return. The Van Wagenens had to pay Dumont for both Isabella and Sophia. They paid $20 for Isabella and $5 for Sophia. The Van Wagenens then set them free.

Now free, Isabella began to build her life anew. She found a job as a seamstress and then as a maid. For the first time, people paid her for the work she did. She wanted no part of her former life as an enslaved person. She took the last name of the kind family who had helped her. She became known as Isabella Van Wagenen.

An 1840 poster listing a reward for four fugitives from slavery.

The New York law did not free all the state's enslaved people at once. The younger workers had to remain with their enslavers until they reached their twenties. Isabella had several children. Every one of them, except Sophia, still belonged to Dumont. Isabella had left them behind to gain her own freedom.

An enslaved mother rocking and singing to her baby in their cabin

In late 1826, Isabella learned that her son, Peter, was gone. The Dumonts had given him to a relative, Solomon Gedney, who took Peter to the South. Isabella was furious.

She knew that the Dumonts had broken the law. It was illegal for enslaved people in New York to be sent to the South. They had to stay in the North until they were set free. If Peter was forced to stay in the South, he might be enslaved forever. Isabella could not bear this. She decided to face the Dumonts.

Dumont said he had not known that Gedney would take Peter to the South. He even felt sorry for Isabella. But Mrs. Dumont laughed at her former worker. She thought it was foolish to be so upset about a Black child. To her, Peter was no different than any other property. But Isabella wanted her child back.

Isabella filed and won three lawsuits in her life. The first was to get back her son, Peter. The second time, she sued members of a religious community for talking badly about her. The third time, she sued a Washington DC streetcar conductor who would not let her ride the car and tried to force her out.

With her friends' help, Isabella sued the Dumonts in order to get Peter back. No one believed that she could win a case against a rich, white family. The fact that Isabella, as a formerly enslaved person and a Black woman, felt she should be able to use the justice system showed her courage. It also showed her strong sense of right and wrong.

During the trial in 1828, Isabella's lawyer told Peter's story before a judge. He told the judge how poorly Peter had been treated. Gedney had beaten him. Peter's back, forehead, and cheek were covered with scars. The judge saw that Peter was very frightened. He decided Gedney could not keep Peter. Isabella won her case.

Isabella's belief in God had continued to grow during her fight for Peter. She now believed that God was responsible for her success. Isabella decided to learn more about her religion. She also decided to go to New York City. She knew she could find a better job there. Perhaps one day, she could buy a small house where all her children could live.

In 1828, Isabella and Peter arrived in New York City. Sadly, she had to leave Sophia with her other children at the Dumonts' home. It would be too difficult to work long hours with such young children. Once in New York City, Isabella found work as a maid.

In New York City, Isabella's son, Peter, became a bit of a troublemaker. In 1839, when he was 18, Isabella made Peter join a whaling ship. She hoped that once he was away from the temptations of New York, he would straighten out. After Peter left for sea, Isabella received a few letters, but she never saw him again.

Chapter Four

ON THE ROAD

In 1843, Isabella believed that God appeared to her in a dream. God told her to deliver the messages of the **Gospel** across the land. Isabella gathered the few belongings she had and left the city with just 25 cents. She felt she should change her name again. Isabella was the name she had during her years as an enslaved worker. She did not want it any longer. Isabella was going to sojourn, or travel, to preach the messages of the Gospel. So she changed her name to Sojourner Truth.

Eventually Truth came to a Massachusetts community called Northampton. Members of the community owned and operated a silk mill. They also believed in social equality. They thought people of different skin colors, genders, and religions should all be treated equally. Truth came to think of this community as her home. She said she was allowed "equality of feeling" and "liberty of thought and speech."

Sojourner Truth settled in Northampton, Massachusetts (pictured here), and met other people who strongly opposed slavery.

While in Northampton, Truth met abolitionists for the first time. She realized that the antislavery message the abolitionists preached could be woven into her speeches. When Truth left Northampton, she began including an antislavery message in her preaching. Truth traveled from town

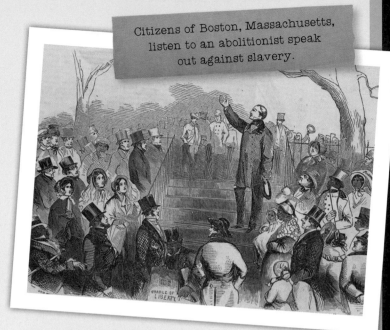

Citizens of Boston, Massachusetts, listen to an abolitionist speak out against slavery.

to town throughout the Northern states to preach the word of God and to speak out against slavery. She went as far west as Missouri and Kansas preaching her message of equality and faith. Many people respected her ideas. They invited her to stay in their homes.

Sojourner Truth captured the attention of her audiences. She was six feet tall and wore a white turban on her head. She carried herself with great pride. She had large muscles from years of hard work. But it was not just her appearance that struck people. Truth's thoughts and ideas impressed many who listened. Her audiences found truth in her arguments against slavery. People listened to her wherever she went.

During that time in the United States, free women did not have the same rights as men. They were considered second-class citizens. Women in the United States were not allowed to vote. **Suffragists** hoped to change this. They worked for a woman's right to vote.

In 1850, Truth joined the women's rights movement and became a suffragist. She believed every U.S. citizen deserved the same rights. In 1851, Truth gave her famous "Ain't I a Woman?" speech to the Women's Rights Convention in Ohio.

Things were not always easy for Truth. Some abolitionists refused to let her join them because she was a woman. Some suffragists refused her because she was Black. Even with these setbacks, Truth kept working for equality.

In 1857, she decided to settle in the town of Battle Creek, Michigan. Many abolitionists lived in this area. Truth joined a religious group and made several new friends. She was 60 years old and wanted a place to call home. Later, some of her children moved to Battle Creek to be close to her.

Like most formerly enslaved people, Truth was illiterate. She had never been taught to read or write. Yet, even without schooling, she was a smart woman.

Women being turned away from a voting location in 1880.

Truth continued to travel and to give speeches. The country was in the midst of a difficult time. Abolitionists were speaking out against slavery more firmly than ever. But the South still did not want to lose the free labor of enslaved workers.

By January 1861, several Southern states **seceded** from the **Union**. More states followed and the **Confederate States of America** was formed. President Abraham Lincoln would not allow the Confederate states to secede from the Union. On April 12, 1861, the U.S. Civil War began.

Sojourner Truth drew crowds when she spoke.

In January 1863, the Emancipation Proclamation freed all the enslaved people living in the Confederate states. But Southerners living there did not consider themselves to be part of the United States. They did not feel they had to follow the president's orders. They refused to free their workers. Millions of enslaved people were forced to work just as they always had.

Sojourner Truth continued to speak out during the war. More and more people came to hear her preach. President Lincoln invited her to the White House. The president respected Truth's views. After her visit, Truth said, "I must say, and I am proud to say, that I never was treated by anyone with more kindness and cordiality than were shown to me by that great and good man, Abraham Lincoln."

The war between the Northern and Southern states continued into 1865. The South finally surrendered on April 9, 1865. In December 1865, Congress passed the Thirteenth **Amendment**. This act formally freed all enslaved people in the United States. But Truth understood that freedom and equality were two different things. There was still much work to be done.

Newly freed men and children in Richmond, Virginia in 1865.

This painting, created around 1893, portrays Abraham Lincoln and Sojourner Truth's meeting.

Chapter Five

AFTER THE WAR

Unfortunately, once enslaved people were freed, whites still did not treat them well. Many people continued to believe that Blacks were inferior. Sojourner Truth still had work to do—both for Blacks and for women. The government **appointed** Truth to the Federal Freedmen's Bureau. This organization helped formerly enslaved people start their lives as free men and women. Truth helped these formerly enslaved workers find land and homes. She worked on fighting Black poverty.

Sojourner Truth in 1864

These suffragists fought for voting rights in the early 1900s, although women weren't granted the right to vote until 1920.

Truth helped Black women learn skills to help them find jobs. In 1868, the Fourteenth Amendment granted Black men the right to vote. Truth knew this was a big step, but women of any color still did not have the right to vote. She continued to work with the suffragists. In 1872, Truth tried to cast a vote in the presidential election. Workers blocked her entrance to the voting booth.

Women were granted the right to vote in 1920 when the Nineteenth Amendment to the U.S. Constitution was passed.

Truth continued to speak in public, but over time, she became ill. She died in Battle Creek in 1883. Truth had not been afraid of death. She believed that God would be with her after she died.

Approximately 1,000 people attended Sojourner Truth's funeral. A well-known abolitionist and suffragist spoke to the crowd. He told everyone about the remarkable woman named Sojourner Truth.

Truth was one of the first Black women to fight for enslaved people's freedom. She was also among the first Black women to fight for a woman's right to vote. Her accomplishments were not always recognized during her lifetime. Nor were her speeches and beliefs always liked. Once, when Truth was preparing to speak in Indiana, someone told her that if she was going to speak there, the building would be burned down. Truth replied, "Then I will speak upon the ashes." Her commitment to social equality never weakened.

The 1986 postage stamp honoring Sojourner Truth

Today, many people have honored Sojourner Truth's name. She is now considered by many to be one of the most important Black women of the nineteenth century, along with Harriet Tubman. In 1986, the U.S. Postal Service designed a postage stamp with Truth's picture. In 1997, NASA launched a probe to study Mars. That probe was named *Sojourner* in honor of Sojourner Truth.

Truth knew that even after the Civil War, the journey to freedom would not come easily or quickly for Blacks. She knew that any social reform took time and commitment. Her strong Christian faith inspired her to continue to speak about equality throughout her life.

In 2016, the U.S. Department of the Treasury announced that during its next security update, the back of the $10 bill will be redesigned to feature Sojourner Truth and other renowned women who fought for equality and voting rights in America. This will mark the first time in over a century that a woman has been pictured on U.S. paper currency.

A statue honoring three pioneers of women's rights, Sojourner Truth, Elizabeth Cady Stanton, and Susan B. Anthony, was unveiled in New York's Central Park in 2020.

The title page includes a quote from Truth that says:
**"Who made your skin white? . . . Who made mine Black?
Am I to blame . . . because my skin is Black?"**
What does she mean by this?
Do you agree with her words?

**A former enslaver had said that Isabella could
do as much farm work as his best male workers.**
Do you believe there are some things that men always do better than women?
Or things that women always do better than men?
Why or why not?

TIME LINE

1790

1820

1840

1850

ca. 1797
Isabella is born
into slavery in
New York.

1826
Isabella escapes
from the Dumonts
with her daughter,
Sophia.

1828
Isabella and her
son, Peter, move to
New York City.

1843
Isabella believes
God appears to her.
She changes her
name to Sojourner
Truth.

1850
Truth becomes
involved in the
women's rights
movement.

1851
Truth gives her
"Ain't I a Woman?"
speech at the
Women's Rights
Convention in
Akron, Ohio.

The first presidential election took place in 1788. An Amendment to the Constitution gave Black men the right to vote in 1868. (Although in many cases Black men were blocked from voting for many years to follow.) It took until 1920 for women to be able to vote. What does this say about who holds the power in the United States, and their views of each group?

Explain the contributions that Truth made to the world. Why were these contributions so important?

1860

1861
The U.S. Civil War begins.

1865
Congress passes the Thirteenth Amendment, which frees all enslaved people in the United States.

1880

1883
Truth dies in Battle Creek, Michigan, in her mid-eighties.

1980–1999

1986
The U.S. Postal Service releases a Sojourner Truth postage stamp.

1997
NASA launches the *Sojourner* probe to study Mars; it is named to honor

2000s

2016
The U.S. Treasury announces it will feature Sojourner Truth on the back of the $10 bill.

abolitionist (ab-uh-LISH-uh-nist)
An abolitionist was a person who worked to end slavery. Truth became an abolitionist after she was freed from slavery.

amendment (uh-MEND-munt)
An amendment is a change that is made to a law or legal document. The Thirteenth Amendment to the U.S. Constitution ended slavery in the United States.

appointed (uh-POYN-ted)
if someone is appointed, he or she is selected for a job. The government appointed Truth to the Federal Freedmen's Bureau.

Christian (KRISS-chin)
A Christian is a person whose religion is based on the life and teachings of Jesus Christ. Truth was a Christian.

Confederate States of America (kun-FED-ur-ut STAYTS of uh-MAYR-ih-kuh)
The Confederate States of America were the Southern states that withdrew from the United States during the U.S. Civil War. The Confederate States of America formed after those states seceded from the Union.

dialect (DY-uh-lekt)
A dialect is a way language is spoken in an area or by a group of people. Frances Gage's account of Truth's "Ain't I a Woman?" speech used Black dialect.

Gospel (GOSS-pull)
The Gospel consists of the books of the Bible that describe the teachings and life of Jesus Christ. Truth preached the Gospel.

illiterate (il-LIT-ur-it)
When people are illiterate, they cannot read or write. Truth was illiterate.

inferior (in-FEER-ee-ur)
If something is inferior, it is not as good as something else. Blacks were often made to feel inferior to whites.

plantations (plan-TAY-shunz)
Plantations were large farms that were usually in the South. Enslaved people often worked on plantations.

seceded (sih-SEE-ded)
If something or someone formally withdraws from a group, it has seceded. The Southern states seceded from the Union before the Civil War began.

suffragists (SUF-ruh-jists)
Suffragists were women and men who worked for women's right to vote. Truth was an outspoken suffragist.

Union (YOON-yun)
The Union refers to the states that stayed loyal to the U.S. government during the U.S. Civil War. The Union army fought against the Confederate army in the war.

BOOKS

Housel, Debra J. *Sojourner Truth: A Path to Freedom.*
Huntington Beach, CA: Teacher Created Materials, 2011.

McDonough, Yona Zeldis. *Who Was Sojourner Truth?* New York, NY: Scholastic, 2015.

Schmidt, Gary D. *So Tall Within: Sojourner Truth's Long Walk Toward Freedom.*
New York, NY: Henry Holt & Co., 2018.

Susienka, Kristen. *Sojourner Truth.* New York, NY: PowerKids Press, 2020.

Turner, Ann Warren. *My Name Is Truth: The Life of Sojourner Truth.*
New York, NY: Harper, 2015.

WEBSITES

Visit our website for links about Sojourner Truth:

childsworld.com/links

*Note to Parents, Teachers, and Librarians: We routinely verify our Web links to make sure
they are safe, active sites—so encourage your readers to check them out!*